0 1 2 3

Write the correct num

0 1 2 3 4 5 6 7 8 9 10

How many pets?
Write the numerals in the boxes.

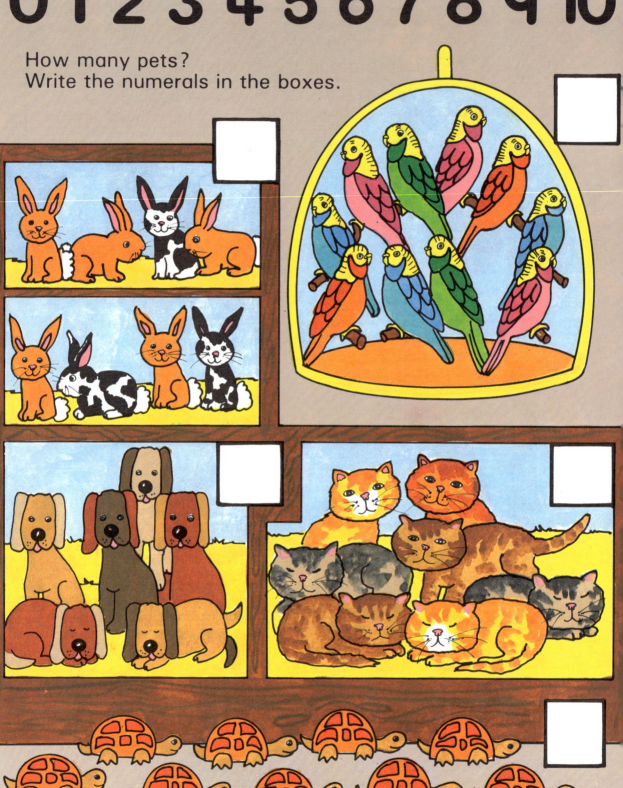

Draw a line to join the words and numerals to the correct number of spots on the cards.

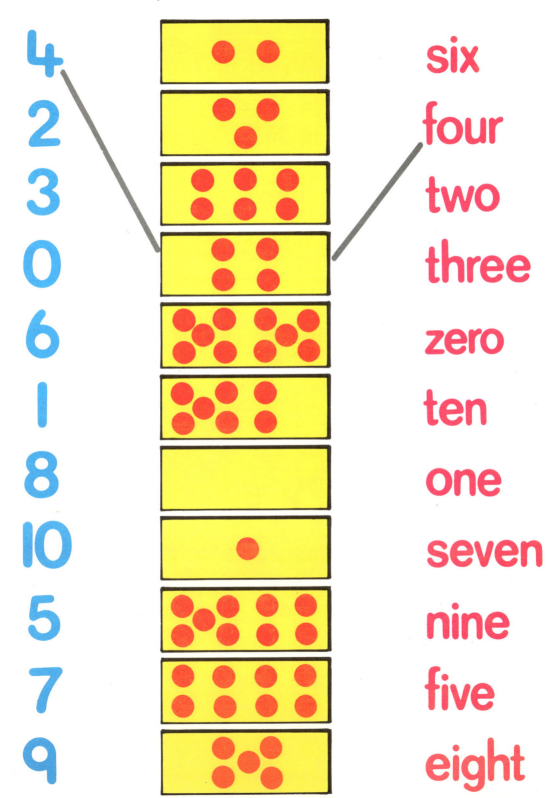

4
2
3
0
6
1
8
10
5
7
9

six
four
two
three
zero
ten
one
seven
nine
five
eight

Write the missing numerals in the spaces on each tape measure.

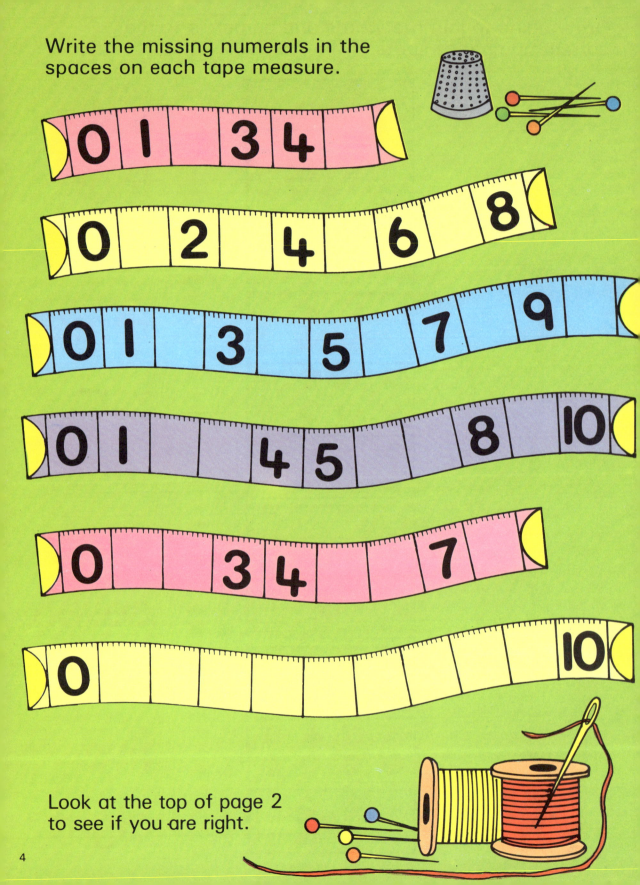

0 1 _ 3 4 _

0 _ 2 _ 4 _ 6 _ 8

0 1 _ 3 _ 5 _ 7 _ 9 _

0 1 _ _ 4 5 _ _ 8 _ 10

0 _ _ 3 4 _ _ 7 _

0 _ _ _ _ _ _ _ _ _ 10

Look at the top of page 2 to see if you are right.

4

How many **more**?
Match the things in the sets to see how many **more**.

How many starfish? 4   How many shells? 3

Example

How many **more** starfish than shells? 1

How many spades? ☐

How many buckets? ☐

How many **more** spades than buckets? ☐

How many sandcastles? ☐

How many flags? ☐

How many **more** flags than sandcastles? ☐

How many balls? ☐

How many bats? ☐

How many **more** balls than bats? ☐

5

How many **less**?
Match the fish in the tanks to find how many **less**.

Example

How many fish? 3　How many fish? 4

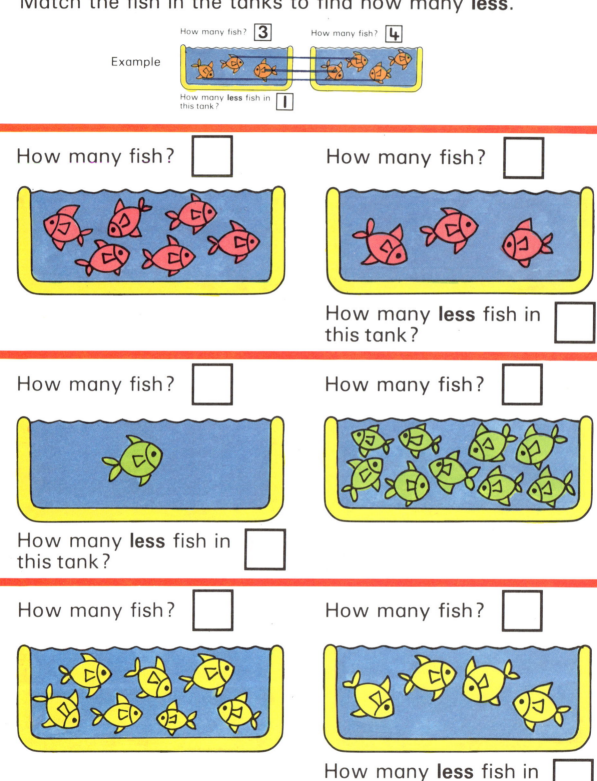

How many **less** fish in this tank? 1

How many fish? ☐　　　How many fish? ☐

How many **less** fish in this tank? ☐

How many fish? ☐　　　How many fish? ☐

How many **less** fish in this tank? ☐

How many fish? ☐　　　How many fish? ☐

How many **less** fish in this tank? ☐

Tell the story

1 egg

3 eggs

2 **more** eggs

1 **less** egg

3 eggs

How many eggs altogether?

Did John find an egg for each friend?

7

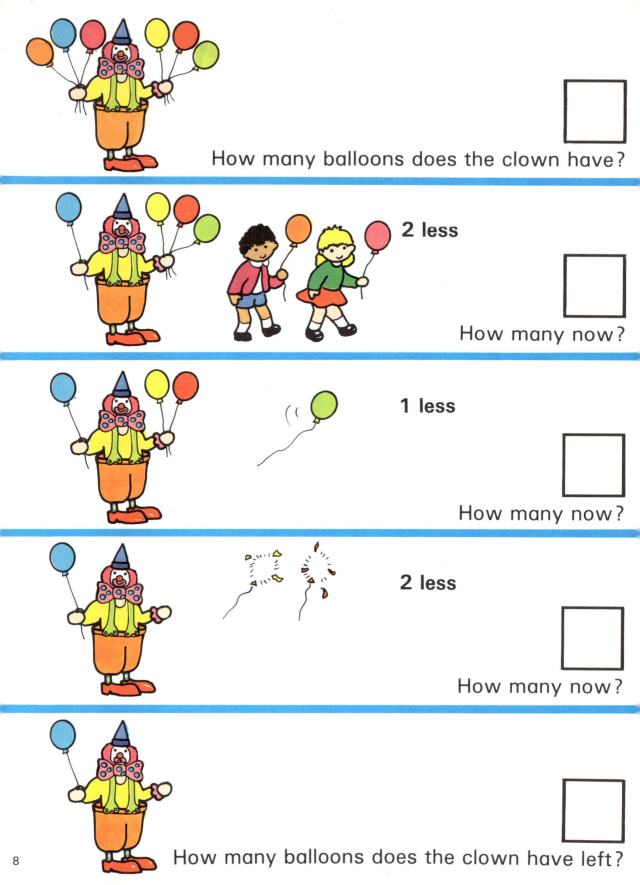

How many balloons does the clown have?

2 less

How many now?

1 less

How many now?

2 less

How many now?

How many balloons does the clown have left?

8

0 1 2 3 4 5 6 7 8 9 10

Add **one** more.
Write the correct numeral in each box.

 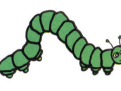 

one caterpillar   **and one more**   How many altogether?

three frogs   **and one more**   How many altogether?

five beetles   **and one more**   How many altogether?

two snails   **and one more**   How many altogether?

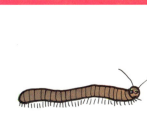 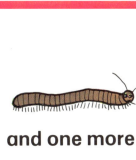 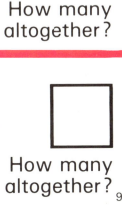

four centipedes   **and one more**   How many altogether?

0 1 2 3 4 5 6 7 8 9 10

Add more.
Write the answer in the box.

four hedgehogs

4

and

two hedgehogs

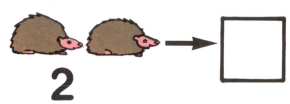

2

six bees

6

and

one bee

1

three butterflies

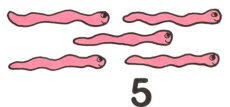

3

and

five butterflies

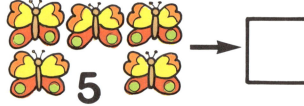

5

five worms

5

and

four worms

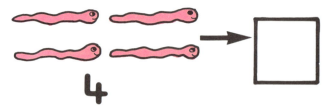

4

two birds

2

and

three birds

3

Add
When we **add** more we use this symbol

3 chicks   **add**   **3** more chicks

We can write this as

3 + 3

Can you **add** these?

Write the correct numeral in the box when you have **added** the two groups together.

2 lollipops **add**   **6** lollipops, is the same as [ ] lollipops.

3 ices   **add**   **4** ices, is the same as [ ] ices.

11

How many flowers?
Write the answers in the boxes.
Follow the symbols. The pictures will help you.

Remember ✚ means **add** on more.

0 1 2 3 4 5 6 7 8 9 10

Add
Write the answer in each box.

Zero

What happens when there are **no more** to add on?
Write the answer in each box.

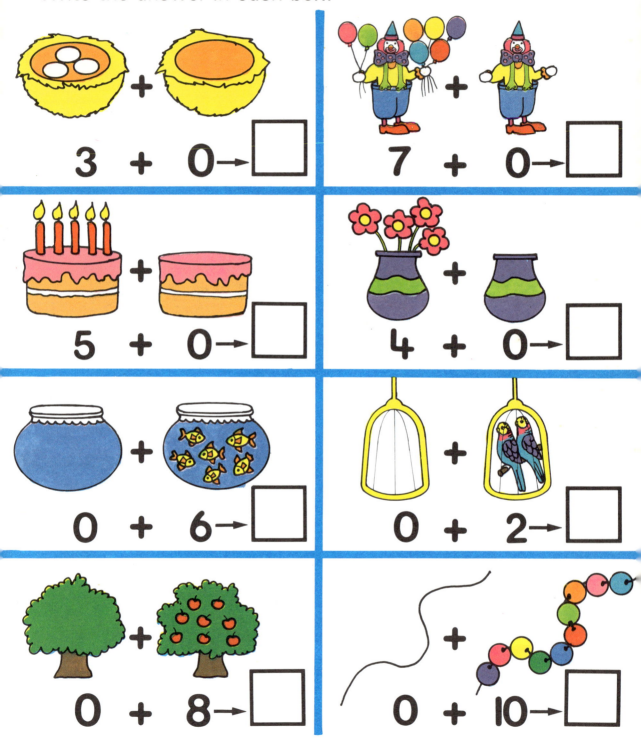

3 + 0→ ☐

7 + 0→ ☐

5 + 0→ ☐

4 + 0→ ☐

0 + 6→ ☐

0 + 2→ ☐

0 + 8→ ☐

0 + 10→ ☐

14 Did you find that the number of things stays the same?

Adding to make 5

Write the correct numeral in each box.

Adding to make 6

Write the correct numeral in each box.

Adding to make 7

Write the correct numeral in each box.

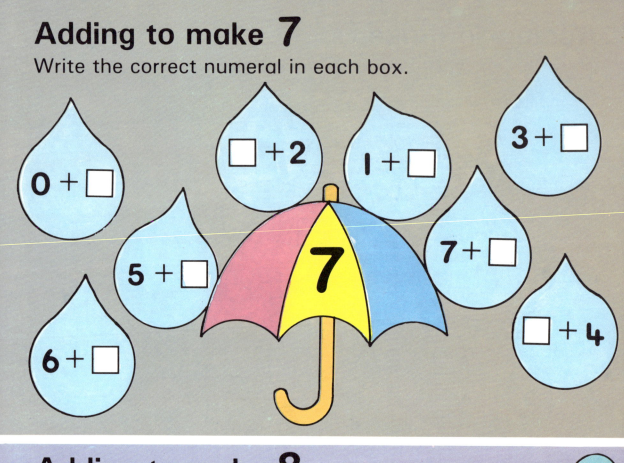

$0 + \square$

$\square + 2$

$1 + \square$

$3 + \square$

$5 + \square$

$7 + \square$

$6 + \square$

$\square + 4$

7

Adding to make 8

Write the correct numeral in each box.

$\square + 1$

$8 + \square$

$\square + 5$

$4 + \square$

$\square + 7$

$0 + \square$

$\square + 3$

$6 + \square$

$2 + \square$

8

Making 9

Now can you make 9?
Write the correct numeral in each box.

$1 + \boxed{} \rightarrow 9$ $\boxed{} + 3 \rightarrow 9$

$\boxed{} + 8 \rightarrow 9$ $\boxed{} + 9 \rightarrow 9$

$\boxed{} + 2 \rightarrow 9$ $4 + \boxed{} \rightarrow 9$

$5 + \boxed{} \rightarrow 9$ $7 + \boxed{} \rightarrow 9$

$9 + \boxed{} \rightarrow 9$ $\boxed{} + 6 \rightarrow 9$

Making 10

Write the correct numeral in each box.

$5 + \boxed{} \rightarrow 10$ $\boxed{} + 1 \rightarrow 10$

$\boxed{} + 10 \rightarrow 10$ $6 + \boxed{} \rightarrow 10$

$2 + \boxed{} \rightarrow 10$ $10 + \boxed{} \rightarrow 10$

$\boxed{} + 4 \rightarrow 10$ $\boxed{} + 8 \rightarrow 10$

$\boxed{} + 7 \rightarrow 10$ $9 + \boxed{} \rightarrow 10$

$3 + \boxed{} \rightarrow 10$

Equals
When we see a sum like this:

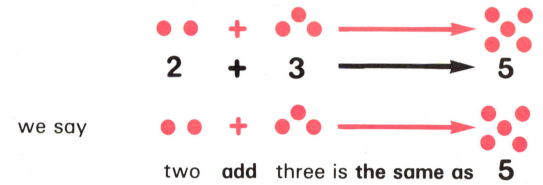

$$2 + 3 \longrightarrow 5$$

we say

two **add** three is **the same as** 5

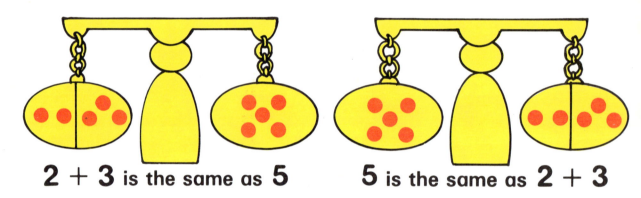

2 + 3 is the same as 5   5 is the same as 2 + 3

When we say **is the same as** or **equals** we can use a
symbol like this ▬

$$2 + 3 = 5$$

Write the **symbol** =

Example $5 + 1 = 6$

2 + 2		4
6		3 + 3
1 + 0		1

$+$ means **add**

$=$ means **is the same as** or **equals**

Write the missing **symbol** or **numeral** in these sums.

$2 + 3 = \Box$

$4 \; \Box \; 1 = 5$

$6 = \Box + 3$

$5 + 5 \; \Box \; 10$

$8 = 6 + \Box$

$2 + 7 \; \Box \; 9$

19

Count down

Count down from the top and fill in the missing numerals.

Match the sets and find the difference.

Example

Jack has **4** books

Jill has **2** books

How many **more** books does Jack have?

2

Jill has **6** mice

Jack has **3** mice

How many **more** mice does Jill have?

The farmer has **9** chicks

Jack has **4** chicks

How many **more** chicks does the farmer have?

Mrs Brown bakes **5** cakes

Jill bakes **4** cakes

How many **more** cakes does Mrs Brown bake?

Take away

There were **6** lettuces

A rabbit eats **1**

How many lettuces left?

There were **9** bananas

A monkey takes **2**

How many bananas left?

There were **8** carrots

A donkey eats **2**

How many carrots left?

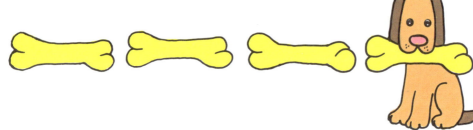

There were **4** bones

The dog takes **1**

How many bones left?

Take away

5 fish   **take away**   **3** fish = ☐ fish

7 fish   **take away**   **4** fish = ☐ fish

9 fish   **take away**   **2** fish = ☐ fish

6 fish   **take away**   **0** fish = ☐ fish

23

Take away

When we **take away** we can use a symbol like this ━
Write the correct numeral in the box.

$$7 - 4 = \boxed{}$$

$$8 - 3 = \boxed{}$$

$$4 - 2 = \boxed{}$$

$$5 - 1 = \boxed{}$$

Take away
Write the answer in each box.

$9 - 7 =$ ☐

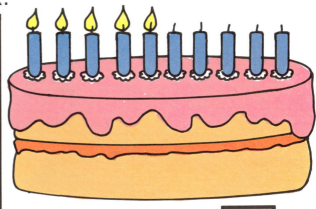

$10 - 5 =$ ☐

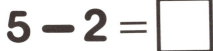

$5 - 2 =$ ☐

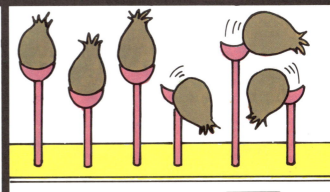

$6 - 3 =$ ☐

$7 - 2 =$ ☐

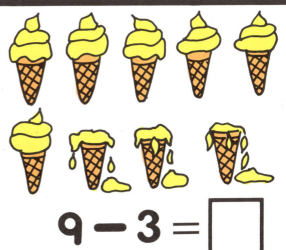

$9 - 3 =$ ☐

25

How many parcels are left?

4   —   2   =   ☐

How many apples are left?

6   —   3   =   ☐

How many bananas are left?

7   —   4   =   ☐

How many bottles are left?

5   —   3   =   ☐

Take away
Write the answer to each of these sums in the cloud shape.

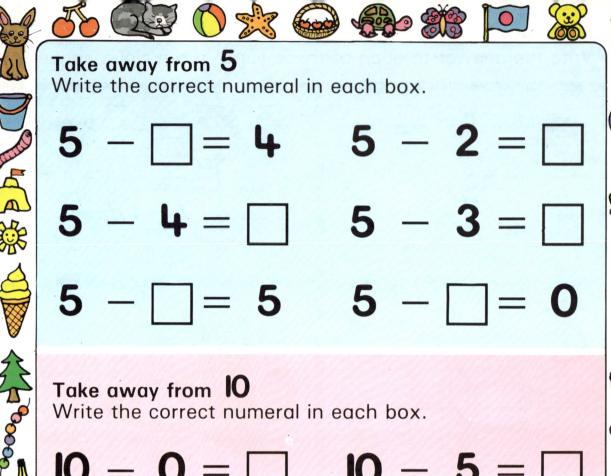

Take away from 5
Write the correct numeral in each box.

$$5 - \boxed{} = 4 \qquad 5 - 2 = \boxed{}$$

$$5 - 4 = \boxed{} \qquad 5 - 3 = \boxed{}$$

$$5 - \boxed{} = 5 \qquad 5 - \boxed{} = 0$$

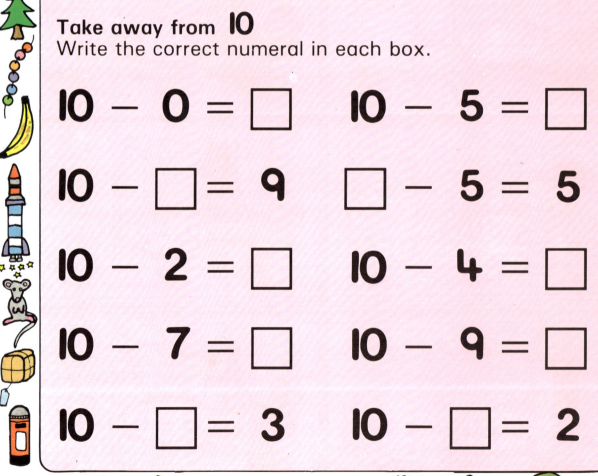

Take away from 10
Write the correct numeral in each box.

$$10 - 0 = \boxed{} \qquad 10 - 5 = \boxed{}$$

$$10 - \boxed{} = 9 \qquad \boxed{} - 5 = 5$$

$$10 - 2 = \boxed{} \qquad 10 - 4 = \boxed{}$$

$$10 - 7 = \boxed{} \qquad 10 - 9 = \boxed{}$$

$$10 - \boxed{} = 3 \qquad 10 - \boxed{} = 2$$

Now practice all that you've learned.
Follow the symbols and write the correct numeral in each box.

$5 + 3 = \boxed{}$ $5 + \boxed{} = 10$

$6 - 0 = \boxed{}$ $3 - 3 = \boxed{}$

$2 + 7 = \boxed{}$ $8 + 0 = \boxed{}$

$\boxed{} + 3 = 4$ $9 - 4 = \boxed{}$

$7 - 5 = \boxed{}$ $10 - 7 = \boxed{}$

$5 - 5 = \boxed{}$ $\boxed{} + 6 = 9$

$7 + 3 = \boxed{}$ $2 - 1 = \boxed{}$

$1 - \boxed{} = 0$ $4 + 6 = \boxed{}$

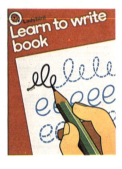

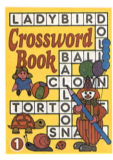

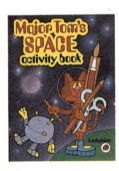
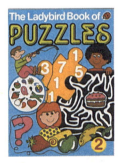

Activity Books
from Ladybird

Series S703
Playbooks

Series S779
Colouring Books
Dinosaurs
ABC
Steam Trains

Series S812
Learn to write
I can write
Crossword Book 1
Puzzles Book
Learn to Count
General Knowledge Quiz Book
Learn to do sums
Learning to read
Learning the alphabet
Times tables
Nursery rhyme abc
Shapes and colours
Tell the time

ISBN 0-7214-3086-4

70p
net

Printed in England